A Look Inside

by
Steven James Schuette

Cover and Illustration by
Natalie Forster

Published by Golden Pillar Publishing, P.O. Box 2531, Elk Grove, California, 95759. http://www.goldenpillarpublishing.com

ISBN 1-890305-56-1

First printing in paperback edition, 2002.
Printed in the United States of America.

Biography

S teven J. Schuette, born September 15, 1972, in Sheboygan, Wisconsin to James and Mary Schuette. He was the third of four brothers. Steven attended Sheboygan Falls Elementary and Middle School, and graduated from Sheboygan Falls High School in 1991. In 1999, Steven Schuette was married to Rebecca, nee Gross and in 2002 was expecting their first child. In his spare time, Steven enjoys writing, spending time with family and friends, and working on his computer.

Steven Schuette, a native of Sheboygan Falls, Wisconsin, graduated from Cardinal Stritch University in Milwaukee, Wisconsin receiving a Masters of Business Administration and a Bachelors of Management Information Systems, and a German Certification from the University of Wisconsin-Platteville.

Steven Schuette's poetry has been published in the following anthologies: *The Poets Anthology* – by CERA; *Dimensions of Thought* – by the Poetry Guild; *Treasured Poems of America Summer 1998*, *Treasured Poems of America Winter 1998*, *The Years of Excellence 1988 – 1998* – by Sparrowgrass Poetry; *Dawn of Silence*, *Outstanding Poets of 1998*, *A Symphony of Verse*, *A Whispering Silence* – by National Library of Poetry; and *American At the Millennium The Best Poems and Poets of the 20th Century* – by the International Library of Poetry.

Preface

This is a book of poetry compiling what I have written over the past 15 years. It illustrates how my writing has grown and changed during this time, as well as some of the periods that I went through in my life. Writing poetry has always been an emotional and almost therapeutic release for me, and some of the poetry is very dark and depressing—a reflection of what I was going through at that time—and others are very upbeat and 'fluffy' if you will. My writing has changed, as I have gotten older. Some are simple pieces, others are full blown; some pieces may or may not have rhyme to them, other pieces just don't follow the 'norm'.

The book is portraying the incidents that happened in my life and the feelings I felt. They represent the obstacles of my life, and the trials and tribulations that I went through during those times. I end the book with a compilation of the names of my family members, using their name to describe the person they have become.

Steven J. Schuette

Acknowledgments

Writing to me is a solitary process—just me and my favorite beverage—however revising and editing this book is a social one. I would like to thank the people that have taken time to read my work and offer comments and criticism; you have helped me tremendously. In addition, I would like to thank those positive influences on my life. My parents are probably the two biggest influences in my life. Also my wife, who has stood by me since I began and encouraged me to write what I feel and not conform to standards. I would like to thank my entire family for the support and encouragement they have given as well as some ideas for my writing. And finally, my close friends—you know who you are...Thank you.

Table of Contents

My Family

A Look Inside

Pressure

Pressure mounts
tension pulls
stress is too much
what do you do?
Pressure increases
tension strikes
stress grinds
what happens now?
Pressure, tension, and stress
are all problems,
People do not realize
how divesting these problems
actually are.

Watching

Watching people
is a way for them
to define themselves
to display
actions, feelings, and emotion
it is a way
for them
to form opinions of others
for them
to form thought
later to remember all
to use to help
help in forming
the figure in your mind.

Boredom

Sitting in your room
not actually knowing why
wondering what to do.
Understanding there is nothing to do
nothing at all.
So you sit there,
and sit there,
and sit there,
starting to go out of your mind.
Why?
Why you ask.
The reason is because
you are so bored.

Time

Time flys
when you are having fun,
time stands still
when you are bored.
What happens to time
when you are waiting.
Time is
to fast for what must be done;
to slow for nerves,
just right for a meeting.
So what do you say
about time while waiting.

Messages

Messages
meaningful or not
you will not know
till it is read.
Messages
good or bad
only you'll know
whether or not.
Messages
long or short
boring or not
who knows,
important
you may hope so.
Messages
you will only know
if you actually read them.

Children

Children so small,
so adorable,
yet so noisy;
How can something
so small,
so cute,
be so loud?

Work Work

Work work
also called torque.
For me it is too much
and never enough.
You always leave
wearing short sleeves.
Then you work
with a spoon and fork.
Then you go home
only to hear the phone.
Again they need you
Oh Boy I'm a fool.

Instructors

They teach you everything,
or so they say.
They yell, they scold
only to better your chances
in the real world.
They help, teach,
and show others a path;
a path in which
is the easiest and the best
for that student.
The path in which
the students show his/her strengths.
In a chance to,
well to perfect his/her chances,
his/her chances in the real world.

Steven J. Schuette

Life: A Partial Starting

Have you ever felt
that you were always left out.
People tease you,
and you feel like a fool.
Out of place here
with no one near
who will take you
for whom you are, not a fool.
You wish you could fit in
with everyone, even him.
You wish you weren't so uptight,
but that's all right.
You really wish you could fit in,
but you know you'll never win.
Trying to be something you're not,
but what you want
is to be it,
and not a twit.
You wish people would include you,
but then you'd loose your cool.
You always feel out of place
when you look into their face.
You wish it were easy,
but life is not easy.
Everyone makes it look so easy and fun,
but what happens when up comes the sun.
Then comes the end.
For it all to start again.

Parents

The glitter of life
starts with your parents
For you and I.
We know that, or do we?
Some kids disregard their parents,
others ignore, slander, or torture their parents;
but do they realize
how much parents are there,
how much they actually care.
No one really comprehends
a parent's love
except for the parents themselves.
Sure we think we know,
but we kids don't.
We hate our parents when they yell,
love our parents when they compliment us,
and ignore our parents when uninterested;
but we never realize what they go through.
The torture of love,
of punishment, of disagreement, and of ignorance.
They love us all life long,
and even after death (theirs or ours).
They love us the same;
no matter if twins, triplets, or a single child.
Their love never ends,
and maybe that is our problem.
We never realize how hard it is,
to let go of something you love with all your heart.
And someone you
never want to leave.

Steven J. Schuette

Nervous

Nervous,
the foot always twitching.
Nervous,
the hands always moving.
Nervous,
the person never sitting still.
Nervous,
you know the mind is wondering.

Why am I so nervous?
Why are they nervous?
Who knows!
Surely not I!
Maybe you?
Oh no, I'll never know,
because I'm too nervous to ask.

Gladness

Gladness is
when flowers loose their blooms
and trees their leaves,
Gladness is
fog lying on the fields
And frost in the air
Gladness
Lives in the heart of God.

What a Day!

Have you wanted to be someone else,
a cat, a dog, or even a mouse.
Well that is how it is
for a guy who's a whiz.
You go to school,
but you're a fool.
You're always put down
until you frown.
Then they tease
until you leave.
Afterwards they laugh
until the bell rings for the next class.
But that's not it
until you quit.
Then you've lost
at your own cost.

Sunset's Color

The color
red, orange, and yellow
so bright and loud
every night
shown all over the world
the colors everyone
knows and appreciated.
The color of a sunset.

Journal of Life

Do you ever feel like the odd ball of the school?

You walk into school
everyone stares at you.
You go to your locker
everyone becomes a mocker.
People criticize the changes in you
even though you've changed all through school.
You grow your hair longer,
the mocking becomes stronger.
You're considered a nerd,
so everyone's heard.
Well that's how it is
for a guy who's a wiz.
Trying to fit in,
but he knows he'll never win.

Vision of Innocence

Sitting there
a vision of innocence
she tries
but not sure of the ropes
up she goes
but to short to reach
so
content where she is.

The First Day

The first day
What was it like?
People inquire
Why do they ask,
only they know.
Wow you think
only 364 left!
You think to yourself
Thank God there is only one
First Day,
You begin by
entering a building
knowing nothing
and no one.
It is so hard
on the first day.
So much to learn,
so much to pick up on,
and so many people
to get to know.
Wow, Thank God there
is only one First Day.

Little Children

Small, cute, and compact
How can something so small
hold so much?
They hold much.
Their parent's love
as well as the love of others.
So young
yet so precious,
so adorable,
yet irreplaceable
It is unbclicvable
how parents can create
something so precious
so....
out of this world.

Silence

Silence
the deadly killer
memories float around
shoving knives into your heart.
Then confronting those fears
that will up and flow with the silence
that was so nice to hear
will the silence ever come back
do I ever want it to return.

Homecoming

The day is here,
a day to cheer.
School is out,
everyone shouts.
People moan today,
when they must walk in the parade.
But that's O.K.,
because today's the day.
When everyone is cheerful,
and very fearful.
Because tonight is homecoming game,
just the same.

Searching

The eyes hold so much.
Explanations, answers, truth,
and much more,
So while searching
check in the eyes
you will find
what you are looking for.

Steven J. Schuette

Job

A job
fun or boring
only you can answer.
To some it is fun
to other it is work
yet to others it is boring.
A job is only what you make of it
fun only if you make it fun,
and boring only if you make it boring.
It is up to you
on how to judge a job.
Like they say,
you cannot judge a book
by its cover,
nor can you judge
a job by its appearance alone.

Reflect

Reflecting image
was it even real
or just another image
mirrors reflect something
real or fake
the image
is a fake
backward but with all details
details seen in a different light.
Is it the same?

Work

Work what a word!
Who ever came up
with a word so strenuous,
a word so hard.
Boy! what would it be
if the word work meant something
totally different.
Wow! what a thought
A thought, only in reality
work means work,
and according to some
is a nasty four letter word.

Phone Calls

Phone calls
annoying, worth while
how would you know
unless you answer.
But why answer if annoying.
These are petrifying questions
and only you can make the decision
of whether to answer the phone or not
Do and you may get annoyed,
upset, or even depressed;
do not and you may
miss an important call
miss a lonely voice
or even mess up an important deal.
Phone calls.

Steven J. Schuette

The Word Death

Death
wow what a word
what a depressing word
Do you not wonder
wonder why God ever
created such a word.
Why do we die
we know we cannot
live forever
but why hurt so many
when you leave.
Why could not
such a short word
be easier to comprehend
to understand
and to handle.
Why why
I do not know.
I wish I did.

The Real Meaning

Sounds so sweet
means so much
yet the words
are never heard
the melody and music
the singer and auditions
cover the words
cover the real meaning.

Ponder

Sitting staring into space
a black curtain appears
then a picture
my head bobs
my mind wonders
thoughts; I know not why;
appear out of thin air
a voice inside
says wait
where are we
not where we should be
but not where I'd want to leave
so I stay
until an outside force
starts to pull me back
to reality and the real world
only to postpone the ending
until the next time
that black curtain falls
only to rise again.

Visitors

Having a visitor
can be
fun, boring, hectic, or relaxing
no one knows
until you have a visitor yourself
and then get to know it.

Steven J. Schuette

A Right Answer

re a right answer?
ks, you answer,
feel guilty
g the truth
hat seems
she wanted to hear.
speak up?

y
ou were raised.
erstand
blem

ye   wedge in a relationship
or ju   tion.
Guilty i.   el,
but relieved
I answered the truth
that is what is important.

A Pain

A pain that never subsides
one word
triggers tears
one song
triggers hurt
one sight
triggers misbelieve
feelings that hurt so much

The Decision

The decision
is right,
right for who.
It is logical,
but very unthoughtfull.
You wonder
why was it made,
bad for business,
since when,
hinders production
says who,
but the decision
was made.

Picture's Mixture

The mixture of colors
that forms a thing
is so unbelievable.
The colors
are brought together
together to form what
only the one looking
can tell truly what it forms.

Pests and Pals

Pests and pals
they can be one.
One can be a pest,
but at the same time can be a pal.
Your best friend
could be a pest,
and then again could be a pal.
Not all are both
but do not get discouraged
if they happen to be both.
Being a pest,
and at the same time a pal
is good
it keeps others on their toes
keep them alive
and in the real world.

Last Night

Last night I cried myself to sleep
wondering where you were
remembering the past
and the future we had made
finally falling asleep
My pillow dripping.

Money

Money the root of all evil
Is it really? Yes or No.
To some people
money is number one,
to others
money means nothing.
Does that mean
people to whom it is number one
are evil,
NOT.
Money
helpful, harmful
money is what you make of it.
Evil harmful to those who
use it against others,
or to harm others.
Good helpful to those who
use it to better others
or even themselves.
Money if good,
could be harmful.
Good to one person
harming others at the same time.
So is Money
really the root of all evil?

Steven J. Schuette

Life: Sophomore

Life now,
you thought freshman was hard
just wait.
It really may not be harder
just more complex.
You have adjusted to
on campus life,
study skills,
and working habits.
Being a Sophomore
is easier and yet harder;
you understand campus life
in that sense easier,
but the classes are harder.
Sophomore life
is overall easier
you already know
know your way
around campus and
how to better yourself.

Life: Freshman

Morning
how painful;
Life as a freshman
changes a person.
You learn to be
well to be on your own
with no one forcing you
to do
your homework
or studying.
It is up to you
Freshman learn to create
study habits and relationships.
Being a freshman
teaches you how to live
on your own.
One thing to remember
is to have fun and enjoy it.

Steven J. Schuette

College

College
wow what a word
One moment you are on the top
next you are back on the bottom,
but worse
this is all new,
you are on your own.
You live the way you want to
do what you want
and when you want to do it.
This step is very scary
the thought of jumping into something
you really know nothing about
something that has so many questions
why? how? when? where? what? etc.
Things seem all scary and new
until it begins
then you notice
it is like
like just starting over
in high school again
just different land.

New Day

Starting off a new day
in a manner,
a manner in which is new to all
is fun on occasion,
different on occasion,
real on occasion
and needed on occasion.
Starting off a new day
is a time to begin impressions and ideas
ones of good nature,
ones of bad nature,
and ones that do not matter.
Starting off a new day
is new to all.

Loneliness

Loneliness is there,
but never seen;
it is thought of,
but never heard
why why why.
Why ask why
the answer to that is all inside
each individual,
each person.
Everyone feels
in different ways
using different styles
at different times.

Steven J. Schuette

Being An Outcast

Being an outcast
not fitting in
listening understanding
but not talking
sitting alone
quite, lonely
afraid to say
to say anything.
Being an outcast
sitting in the corner
seen, ignored
no one comes to see,
to check how he is
or if he is fine
no one comes
no one at all.
Being an outcast
people talk behind your back
slander flying
without proof
no way to save
your untouched name
which is now
topic of all discussion.
Being an outcast
no one wants to talk
about things you know
conversation to high
understood, but not interested
feeling unwanted, being unwanted.
Being an outcast.

Concur The Day

Sitting there
staring aimlessly
you feel your body
begin to float
your mind wonders
to unknown places
yet you are relaxed
calm and collected.
Upon return
you feel energized
rejuvenated
and ready to
concur the day.

Faceless

An image
appears over and over
yet each time
incomplete
the longing in your heart
never ends
for one day
you'll find
the piece
to match
the image in your dreams.

Steven J. Schuette

Crowded

Twelve people one room one bed
wow what a thought.
The word sex, said explicitly
by all inferred
or not
was that an idea of many minds
or words read.
We know not all
yet are now friends
he wants her
but will satisfy her
stroking her hair
while she knows him not
but still does not move
he stares at anything
at…
well use your imagination
but she's not interested
so he moves on
the next also not interested
so he moves on again
finally one's interested
but this one woman
who needs support
is very vulnerable
and is he using her
does he want her
or is he just looking for freebies
well maybe things will work out
but if they don't
he'd better be careful.

Reality of Death

Is it not a frightening thought
of what really happens
when someone dies.
Where do they go
what really happens.
We know that their bodies actually decay,
but what about their soul.
Well I do not know
guess I'll just have to wait
to find that answer.

The Wish

I wish
but wonder how
I know
but wonder why
I want
want it all
I need
need so much
I ask
what about me
I respond
could this be true.

Steven J. Schuette

Depression: [Alone]

Depression is hard, and people never realize
that it hurts and bites when things are said
like you'll get over, but you know that.
That's not your problem.
Your problem is how to, not when.
The problem starts with no one there
to end your despair.
no one there to help you out,
but it's no use the stone dauth not speak.
So you're back where you began
alone with no one home.
Left to conquer depression without anyone to help,
but that's the hardest when you're always left out.
with no one to lean on, nothing to balance on.
With no one behind you giving you a boost.
Again you're all alone.
Sure there are Counselors,
Social Workers and others,
but they're just a bother.
They tell you what's right for you.
but how do they know.
It's your life, not theirs.
So depression rises,
and again you're all alone.
You wish people would understand you.
You wish they kept their pity.
Pity is what you don't need.
A friend is what you need,
but when depressed all you feel is alone.
Alone,
a feeling you wish would just disappear.

Hug of Die

Hug Traci before you leave
or else you're dead
poor sinful Dave.
This woman Traci
with a posture of perfection
a voice so sweet as
to melt a man's soul
making a man who listens
putty in her hands.
The conversation took many turns
but the sweetness and truth were overflowing
One idea, two ideas
will they ever stick to one subject.
First on idiots
then on roommates
oh I just said that
then to men
leave her without a hug and your dead
sinful to do such a dumb thing.
One name thrown out
then to another
from Dave to Garry
men or boys
must be boys
if they do not treat an angel
like she ought to be treated.
Wow next to sex in a restroom
Which one
men's room or women's room
what wow
men are not so squeamish.

Behind Honor

Tears held behind honor
held behind dignity
the reason for emotion
unknown
needed
yet held back
cry
people think you're a wus
hold it in
and the tension builds
climbing to a limit of explosion
but why don't you explode
why can't you break down
you wonder
tears are there
but unable to flow
tears always being held back.

Pain

Pain so deep
hurts so much
things you can not forget
yet in order to move on
you must
why
the only question that comes to mind

The Truth

The truth
hidden in the eyes
is deadly and harmful
the truth
hidden in the eyes
is the enemy
the one thing unable to hide
the truth
hidden in the eyes
is helpful, curing, and needed
the truth
hidden in the eyes
is not always hidden.

Searching (In the Eyes)

In the eyes
lies the truth
present and past.
Searching for the answer
is not always easy
but usually
can be found in the eyes.
Searching for
an answer, an explanation, the truth
is not always necessary,
but takes up time
and energy.

Tears

The words which were spoken hurt so much
like spikes into me
the hurt, the pain, and anger overwhelmed me
No tears came.
The supports of my heart expanding
to capture it all
I can fell the torment as it builds
the flow becomes too much
No tears came.
I look at you and can sense the pain
I wish I could say something
to help the pain vanish
but your walls prohibited that
No tears came.
I hear the noise around me
Others torment now mine
In return I ask nothing
No tears came.
I fear the collapse of my supports
Feelings and emotions pushing
My actions on their own
And yet…
No tears came.

Good Bye

Thoughts flicker in my mind
empty thoughts, frustrating thoughts
no end and yet no beginning
no finish to what has been started
just repetitive thought.
Thoughts happy, sad,
exciting, depressing flood in
a feeling of being trapped in a vice
constantly squeezing with no way out
no end to this traumatic torture.
A feeling of hopelessness, failure
of being unexpected and unwanted
begin to enter cluttering my already crowded mind
crowded with anger, pain,
and of being misunderstood
these cluttering thoughts out power all others
and linger onward
growing stronger ever moment
stronger and stronger
till my mind can not handle it anymore
and the only thought left in which I can think
is to get rid of this squeezing and isolated feeling
clear the fog in my mind
and get rid of it forever, at any cost
but wait, what about them
what will they think
I can not, but I must
they will understand
my rope is now too short to hang on
and I can not support them anymore
they will now have to learn to support themselves

Steven J. Schuette

Your Eyes

Centers of black
surrounded by areas of green and blue
deepen
to anyone who looks beyond.
Searching eyes can see all,
for these eyes hide nothing.
They speak in emotion and not words.
Sending love to all who need it
without the need for anything in return.
These centers in which I gaze
hold a place for me to escape
from all the tortures of every day life.
This place fills my heart
with joy, tenderness, and peace
which now gives me the ability
to move on
while I leave the past behind,
and look into the future
with excitement.

We're Sorry

Tears form as the words come out
words like daggers
piercing to the soul.
"We're Sorry, but"
you fall
your knees no longer able to support you.
The emptiness appears
pain fills your heart.
Why? is the only thought.
You feel you cannot move on,
but you must.

Tears roll down your face.
Everything is in view now,
but yet you can see nothing.
Again they say;
"We're sorry to inform you, but";
these words tear you apart
anger, sadness, pain
pull all at once
till there is nothing left,
but empty pain
emptiness and pain.

Steven J. Schuette

Death of a Loved One

Have you ever been alone,
talking to only skin and bones.
You say a word,
but you're not heard.
You say it again,
and so it began.
You hurt with the pain
nothing to gain.
Only the loss
of being lost.
And no one to share
your great despair,
For that is how it is
for everyone who lives.
That loses someone
espccially a loved one.

Love You

Love
why can't I say it?
I Love you
is it because
I'm afraid of the past
repeating itself
or just because
I'm to scared
of the future
being unknown.

The Eyes

The eyes
so beautiful
so complicated
so unique.
The eyes
tell stories
give answers
tell the truth
and give explanation.
The eye
well there is so much
about the eyes
that we have just started
to explain and find out.
The eyes are just
so immaculate

Sunset's Beauty

So beautiful, yet so mysterious
how can everyone see the beauty
the beauty of a sunset.
Professors tell us
but speak in a language
a language over our heads.
I guess the beauty of a sunset
is all that is needed.
The beauty is all.

Steven J. Schuette

Life of a Rose

The life of a rose
shows the path of real life
You start out small
like a seed
like a baby.
You grow, mature, and beautify
like the budding of a rose
like the growing of a child.
You bud
like the petals of a rose
like the charm of a child.
You open and close
like the petals of the rose
open at day
close at night
like the life of a man
open in joyous time
closed in depression.
You shine
like the color of a rose
like the accomplishments of a man.
You fade
like the wilting of a rose
like the depression of a life
You wither away
like the death of a rose
like the death of a man.

Falling in Love

Falling in love
is special and nice.
The feeling is wonderful,
the sense of being wanted
is overwhelming.
You feel as if she is the only,
the only woman in the world,
You see her as an angel
perfect, beautiful, and loving.
You hear wonderful music,
your life becomes joyous
worth living.
You look forward to her company,
she is all that matters;
but what happen
to your friends
and your family.
Do they fade?
Of course not.
They are always there
just in a different spotlight.
Love now is the main light,
the others
are now the secondary spotlight.
Still there just pushed back

When in love
you still have friends and family
it is just that love
your love
is the most important now.

Who am I looking for?

Who am I looking for?
Is she out there,
or is this a battle that won't be won?
I look for
compassion and intelligence that confesses.
someone with two ears
that more then hear what I say.
with loving arms
to comfort and soothe troubles away.
Outdoors all around us to enjoy
As children in the future somewhere
always and forever
has to care.

Leaning On Someone

Leaning on someone
is necessary and needed.
It helps relax,
let loose:
feelings of anger and pain,
frustration, confusion, and misunderstanding.
Broad shoulders
are what you need
as everyone hopes
it is what you have.
As for you
it is what you are missing
at a time like this.

Love

Love is a word so hard to say,
but meaning so much.
How can one word
so small and short
mean so much,
and be so hard to say.
The reason is because of its meaning.
Love means
well no one can universally define
the meaning of love.
The reason is
the meaning comes from inside each and everyone.
No one can say love is …….
because it differs from one person to another.
When you fall in love
you then know.
Love is then defined only to you.
When in love
is the time the definition comes out.
Until then love is really nothing.

Steven J. Schuette

Walls of Insecurity

Not knowing what is ahead
is frightening
also encouraging,
not knowing what to say
is scary
and courage building,
not knowing who you are
is unheard of
and great.
Not knowing
is…
Well it is split
one good part and one bad part
one discouraging
and one encouraging,
and both parts are helpful.

Endless Thought

She loves me
She loves me not
flower petals used
to find if one's love
loves back
but the flower petal dies
and lives again
just as love could
Love is really an endless thought.
Why Did I Say Yes!

Why did I say yes?
He says he loves me
and I can see it in his eyes,
but that feeling that they say one feels
when in love
I have not felt yet.
I know not why, but I do no want
to throw away something
that I feel comfortable with
so I can't say I don't love him;
but yet I'm unsure.

Steven J. Schuette

Why did I say yes?
They say one can learn the feeling,
but is that true; Is that fair to him
to lure him in, and hold onto him
while yet unsure of my feelings
unsure I love him.
Unsure I could ever love him;
yet holding on until I do.
But who knows if I ever will.

Why did I say yes?
He is so nice, so gentle with me.
He gives me more than I need;
Love, strength, support.
He's that wall to yell at,
that teddy bear to hug,
that shoulder to cry on,
and that person to talk to.
With all this yet I'm unsure.
Unsure about my feelings,
unsure if I could always love him.
So why did I say yes?

Sitting There

Sitting there
that silhouette of perfection
smooth edges perfectly colored and quiet
you don't hear it
and it bothers you not.
Sitting there
the noise annoyance
but yet hilarious
the people funny, and out of tune
but yet great friends
yet you wish you knew them not.
Sitting there
wondering where they learned to sing
that poor woman caught in the middle
"Ah" the only words heard
that woman
alive or dead
wishing she'd be…
well wishing is all she could do.
Sitting there
42 people, 41 seats
do they think we'll fit
42 people, 100 ego's
darn this bus is to small
stop at corner leaving one person off
41 people, 41 ego's
wow, you think he's got a big ego.
Sitting there feeling this feeling
a feeling
oh God help me
trying
still trying
leaving and still trying.

Steven J. Schuette

Perfection

The face
so sweet,
so delicate,
so young
why do men stare.
well take a look
and you'll be staring to.
The voice
so sweet and innocent
yet stern and honest
melodious and harmonious
yet implied
listen and you're hooked
listen and you melt.
The legs
that reach to infinity
silky, sexy, smooth, and perfect
legs of a beauty queen
legs
well look and you'll know.
The hair
rich like gold
long like heaven
swaying in the breeze
the picture of a dream date
the picture of perfection.

She Knows

When you look
into my eyes
my heart
sinks to the floor
You wonder
does she know
can she actually
read what your eyes say
When you look
at me
My body
tenses up.
Again you wonder
does she really know.

You

The smile that greets you
as you draw near.
The personality
that bubbles over
when she talks.
Beauty that
shines brighter
then the moon.
A figure
of heavenly charm.
All this combined
explains the wonder
of you.

Pinch Me

The way she entered
grabbing the attention of every man
wow what a woman
no I mean a lady
That minute of silence
the sight of a beauty queen
as she grew closer one could see the beauty gleaming
through
the outfit was smooth
accentuating all the magnificent parts she had
the curves and all the color set her face apart
her eyes piercing to my soul
melting my insides
her hair swaying as an angel
gold and silky
perfect in every way
"Hello" a word that flowed out of her luscious lips
the word that pierced my soul
a sound so sweet, so unknown, and yet so sexual
wow one in which I'll never forget
the way she moved with grace and honor
holding her head high and proud
the way the dress so silky and sexy
just flowing along with the movement of her body
wow the only words spoken by all who watched
Pinch me, wait no
if I'm dreaming please never let me wake
a dream like this is worth more then life itself
the sight was of a lady
an angel.

Talking

Sitting there
talking to a woman
of such prestige and poise
that one wonders
as to how can she be my friend.
This woman
is understanding, compassionate, comforting
a listener, a shoulder
but best of all
a friend.
She's one you can bear your soul to
yet never worry
that anyone will ever be told.
She's gold in every way,
sexy in a sensuous way,
childish in a funny way,
and powerful in a mystic way.
She's perfect in every way,
she is open honest
yet mysterious and feminine.

Steven J. Schuette

Never Let Me Wake

One who walks into a room
with the fragrance of beauty and charm
lightening everyone's spirits by her presence alone.
One word from her lips melts every man's being,
A miracle, A goddess beauty from head to toe.
Hair of fiery silk; soft and free,
Eyes beautiful like the ocean
with waves crashing in onto my heart,
gentle eyes showing a way to her soul
a place judge free.
The same eyes peering back into your soul
bringing feelings out
you thought you had lost forever.
Eyes of piercing tranquility
cutting right to one's soul and grabbing hold.
Lips of Luscious love
sensuously grabbing your attention.
A face of an angel
a face into which men's gaze becomes lost forever
This person is an outline of sensuous beauty
with a personality unmatchable.
A woman where one glance is never enough
one glance alone is a dishonor
A woman whose voice is of angels singing
whose humor puts a smile on all faces
A woman
in which to know is the highest honor possible
A woman
where in reality words will never be enough
Pinch me, wait no if I am dreaming
then never let me wake.

Feelings

Feelings so intense
you wish they'd stay forever,
but you know better.
Love a word so
hard to say,
you want to be sure.
She said you're great,
but never says love
is it too soon
or just too hard to say
am I pushing too much.
Love
a very difficult word.

Anger

Anger frustration
as it builds inside
is like claws
scraping inside you
one day everything is so clear
then the next
all is a mess
where does one find
the median
the place
of ease and comfort

Steven J. Schuette

Well Hello

Well hello
to a woman
you've met only once
but the impression made
was one that lasts a lifetime.
Well hello
to a woman
whose friendship is so unique
and so appreciated
a friendship of such honor.
Well hello
to a woman
so kind and considerate
so sophisticated and intelligent.
A person
who it is to be an honor
to be acquainted with
and even a higher honor
to know.
Well hello
to a woman
a woman of such honor and prestige
a woman
in which to know is an honor
Well hello there.

Love Builds Bridges

She hurt me so bad;
yet I love her still
Memories of her race through my mind.
Did I make a mistake;
did I mess up my life?
Yet people say you're much happier know,
how do they know?
Could it be true,
if so then why do I feel this way?
She lied to me;
yet I love her so,
though I can not forgive and forget.
Is it bad enough to throw it all away?
Why can I not decide,
why can I not just move on?
She said she loved me;
if so then why did she betray me.
Love is to be special not used and abused,
yet she took my heart,
and crushed it.
Why even with this can I not move on?
Am I so stupid and dense,
too scared and unsure
to be able to move on,
or is it true that love builds bridges
to strong to ever be broken.

No Replacement

Those who care try to keep track
again something goes wrong
The length can never be determined
What a feeling
when I finally see you again.
Best friends back together,
but not for long.
Our paths again part,
me going my way
and you yours.
The miles are growing
as the years go by.
Plans of separating overshadow the future.
What about the past and all the fun we had?
The troubles that follow you always catch up.
Friends that played such a big part in the past,
the future will not be the same without you.
You are the only one for me.
Now that our paths separate and fade
there will be no other
to replace the love and friendship.

Guilt

I know what I am doing is wrong
But my mind leads me on
Continuing alone, fooling myself
Pretending that everything is okay
My heart is wondering what to do
Part wanting to go on
While part knowing it will get hurt
I do not know which way to turn
My heart and mind are confused
Filled with guilt.

Wanted To Say

I just wanted to say
'Thank You'
for all the support
the friendship
and the consideration
you gave me.
We may not be the best of friends
nor may we be very good friends
but just having the chance
to call you friend
is more then enough for me.

Steven J. Schuette

Your Beginning

The smell…., but I remember
the important parts, the truth
You thought I didn't remember
had everything turned
mind, emotion, pain until waking up
I remember hearing it over and over again
running through my head
I can not forget; wish I could turn off the emotions
but deep down I would still care
it tears me apart
I am confused, I understand or so I thought
I am more confused
The truth I got
now I need everything
You now know mine
now I want yours
You hoped I would not remember
I could not forget ever
still confused
Mine grows
for you yours has only just begin
jumping somewhere into mine
with an introduction,
but my pages are now glued together for safety
your warmth and kindness begins to melt the glue
you begin slowly reading page by page
finding a lot hidden by time
opening secret entrances never opened before
careful words wonderful yet painful
penetrate to a page
ripping it out
to be read by no one else
but to always be remembered by you.
My story ends where yours begins.

Well It Did

You stole my heart
and come to find out
you never wanted it.
All you wanted
was to see if it would work
well it did.
You knew I was gullible
and very innocent
why did that not matter
why did you not respect my innocence
you knew I would fall
and when I did it would be forever
why didn't you take that into account.
You made my life hell
To go on was hard
but one thing will never change
and that is
I will always love you.

Steven J. Schuette

Yours or Mine

Anger your enemy or mine
So angry to explode,
but yet calm as can be;
enough anger to rip its head off,
yet all you say is
"Have a good day
Bye bye NOW."
venting anger
it's helpful,
but held in is harmful
yet what's wrong
with one who can not vent
one who suppresses anger
only to please others
one who has no way
to vent anger
no way to rid himself of anger
so it builds one on-top of another
until that time when it is too much
but when will it be
and can one handle that
or will that be his destruction.
Anger yours or mine

Sorry

Sorry
I wasn't there when you needed me
Sorry
I couldn't help you when you needed it most

Is the word sorry
enough
Sometimes it feels right
other times it just feels
to be the wrong word to say.
Yet does this word
express all that one feels;
too much at times
not enough at other times,
but sorry is the only word
that comes to mind.
I'm so sorry.

The Choice

A sound so sweet
brings back memories
of what was
of what could have been
did I make a mistake
or was this the way to go
why is the answer
not available.

Moving On

A song is heard
tears form and well up
why
feelings of despair
overcome an already confused heart
why are things moving on easy
but in reality not
why
listening to what is said
brings back memories
will they always occur
why
please Lord tell me
so I'll be able to move on.

Freedom

Freedom
a word of settlement
a word of joy
a feeling felt
that joyous day
the beginning of my new life.
Ties were broken
beginnings were made
freedom
the feeling first felt
the best feeling
ever felt

It's Over

The words "it's over"
came so quickly and easy
why did it end
things were rough, tight, and uncharted
but we should have been able to work through them
why could we not
fighting always came about
talk was cheap
fighting was inevitable
but if so why did I fall
fall in love that is
why did I fall in love
she was always there
but was she
secrets hidden,
knowledge unknown
supportive not
why did it all end
end for now
end forever.

Steven J. Schuette

Truth

She says she's sorry, but her tone is insincere;
her apology comes from the heart, or is it greed instead.
She still loves me, but the trust is gone never to return;
the apology is nice
and the idea of returning to a dream is wonderful,
but the walls are built again
and for them to fall would be devastating.
After time has began to heal those open wounds
to reopen them would hurt even more.
I moved on into a world where I'm comfortable
a world of my own;
this is a place where I depend on me.
She says she's changed, and in reality we both have;
we learned to be on our own.
She says she is ready to begin again
but I'm not; the hurt runs to deep and to far
for it ever to begin again.
She says she's wrong and able to commit fully
but would or could I ever be ready again.
Starting new over, beginning a life on my own
was very difficult to begin, but I have adjusted
and yes it gets easier as time goes along;
but writing and wanting to talk will take time
not ready yet to face her.
She says she's sure, not looking for a commitment
but somewhere in her words it is different
How can she expect me to just begin again
I can not do that, I will not do that.
Things may have changed with her
and she is cured, oh, and ready to go on she says,
but I am not ready.
My new life and career has begun,

begun on my own.
I need time to repair a broken heart.
Hitting bottom and know trying to climb out is difficult,
but I need time to do it, and on my own
in order to regain my confidence and self-esteem.
She says she's missed me, but says she's having fun
what am I to think.
I know she wants me back, but I can not
I have moved on, on by my own.
It will take a long time to repair the damage caused,
but we will have to do it on our own.
I am not ready to face her in which she is ready to face
me.
Maybe I am just
I do not know
all I know is that I am not,
not ready to open unhealed wounds.
Writing me and telling me she's changed is great
but she needs to realize that all,
I mean all has changed and I' m not ready to meet face to
face.
For me the phone is easier
actually to write would be even easier
at least putting it all on paper would be easier
and if it were read or not that would be fine
over the phone gets worse but bearable
but when you ask to meet face to face
I am not ready.
I tell you that it will take time, yet you reply
"I can drive you back on Saturday".
Did I miss something, or still you do not hear me
you say you have changed,

but so far I myself did not see that
the part of listening to me is still not there
this is one part very important to me
and she knows that so why is she not
when she says she has changed.
Where is the proof? I do not know
the one thing I do know is that I am happy
with where I am
and I am not ready to jump back into something
something that will end up
right back where I am now
so this is the end
end to what seems took a dynasty
after eight years this is all
but this is best
best for both of us.

I Will Always Remember

I will always remember
your tolerance,
your anger,
your bitterness and confusion;
And I will always remember
the way you criticized,
the way you complimented,
the way you always put yourself down.
Yes I will always remember
your intellect,
your talent,
your patience and understanding;
And I will always remember
the way you sang,
the way you helped,
the way you stood on your own feet.
Yes I will always remember
your indecisiveness,
your sweetness,
your mind.
I will always remember
your lovely voice,
your beautiful eyes,
your long blonde hair;
And I will always remember
the way you feel,
the way you felt,
the way you held me so close.
Yes I will always remember
your dainty hands,
your small feet,
your short and lovely little body.

Steven J. Schuette

I will always remember
your kindness,
your thoughtfulness,
your generosity and curiosity;
And I will always remember
the way you smile,
the way you laughed,
they way you talked all night long.
Yes I will always remember
your touch ,
your sigh,
you're always making others laugh;
And I will always remember
the way you looked,
the way you lived,
the way you held yourself so proud.
Yes I will always remember
your softness,
your kisses,
your love.
And Yes I will always remember
YOU!

Petals

She loves me.
She loves me not,
as the petals fall to the ground.
You wonder
is this the way to determine your fate,
your love;
this concept so old
yet so....
Why use flowers
try one then another
to see if the results are the same or not.
Try once more,
but is this effective.
Does this tell what's in one's heart
or is this an easy way out,
out of the tortures of a decision
which weighs so much on one's heart and mind?
She loves me.
She loves me not,
as the petals fall to the ground.

Lost

I feel so lost.
Why
am I a loner,
or just too stupid and weak
to be able to hold onto something so great.
Why can I not start again.
I mean be alone
on my own
depending on me,
but instead I try and ruin a true friendship.
Am I destined to be alone
for the rest of my life,
or wonder aimlessly for eternity.
I don't know maybe dependent is what I am
unable to depend on myself.
Why am I such a loser
weak feeble and yet old.
Why do I feel so lost.

The Tear Forms

Tear form
as she pulls out of the driveway
a feeling of good-bye flows overhead
you feel afraid, scared, and unsure.
This woman you love,
but you ask yourself
how?
You had it once
lost it,
and now have it again
You keep playing the past back again
trying to see how you screwed up,
but are unable to see,
Will this happen again
because you are
to insecure with yourself
tears form
as thoughts of her
race through your mind.

Afraid

Afraid the answer
you gave
is not correct.
You try to be open,
but feel uncomfortable,
why.
This person of beauty and charm
makes you feel so
secure
when she's around,
but then why can't I tell her
everything.
Why can't I be
that person
I've always
wanted to be?
Why why?

Starting Fresh

Starting fresh
right from the beginning
is strange.
The territory is unseen
and the language is scary,
but the freedom and peace
is the best thing to possess.
To loose that
is to loose your own life
your own existence.

An Illusion

Sitting there
wondering what she is thinking.
You fell and fell hard,
but did she notice.
She's beautiful, intelligent, and independent
a perfect woman,
but she believes you not.
You dream of her
in ways that are not normal,
but you are scared
when you're together.
You feel comfortable, warmth, and acceptance
like you've never felt before.
You are scared to loose that
so nothing happens,
but things get closer
feelings begin to change.
You wonder does she feel the same,
or feel anything
or not.
What happened?
She loved me one moment
and then I am alone.
Did I mess up
or was it all just
an illusion.

Steven J. Schuette

Ache In My Heart

An ache in my heart
that proceeds to be present
time after time.
I can not forget her,
I miss her.
People say I'm foolish,
but lonely is more the word
lonely of having someone there;
someone who needed me
needed me to
listen; be strong; hold her.
They say you're lucky.
Lucky yah right,
lucky how.
I put my heart into her for so long
and then this
alone again.
Oh yes! I call that lucky.
To give fully your heart and have it broken
and now scared for your life
and so
there will always be
that ache in my heart.

Misleading

Misleading
the signs, gestures, and words
are very confusing.
She says it one way
then another,
but yet then another.
Is one to stick with the initial thought
or go for the roller coaster ride.
Misleading:
the things you want to hear
are not said,
but yet latter they are.
What is one to think?
Things keep changing
feelings keep going,
but changes.
Feelings of love
become stronger,
but in a different way.
Love as companion
now changes
to love of a brother or sister
actually in the same.
Misleading,
way to misleading.

Steven J. Schuette

Starting Over

Starting over
like crawling
for the very first time
is difficult, scary, and helpful;
people to help
unknown to you.
You feel trapped, caged, and bound
wondering if it'll ever be all right,
but thinking
God help me
I'm shrinking
melting
blending into the background
without a way out.
Wondering if anyone knows
what is happening;
why me;
will it ever end,
or is this the black whole of my life.

Alone

Alone
a feeling of emptiness
a feeling of nothingness
sitting staring at your ceiling
not knowing what to do
or where to go
it's hard
and people do not realize
how much you hurt
how much you care
how much you need someone there.

Thought

Wow what a thought.
When one peers into
a woman's eyes
you see her soul,
or is it your soul you see,
or you see only your reflection;
is it good
is it a sign.
Her soul is so deep
so full of secrets,
yet so beautiful and glorious.
You look some more
feeling yourself being pulled in
pulled into a world unknown to you.
A world you're only too anxious to see.

Steven J. Schuette

Scared

Alone
in an unfamiliar place
yet comfortable and secure;
The surroundings
are peaceful and calm
making my mind wonder.
Alone
in a new environment
unsure of what to do
where to go
so many things
yet unseen,
but too afraid
of moving forward.
Alone yet
with many people around
secure and safe
but scared
scared of the unknown.
Alone,
a feeling present
a lot of the time.

Thank You

How can the words "Thank You"
ever tell you how much
I appreciated the kindness, the gentle hand,
the shoulder, the support
in which you gave out of selflessness
These words can never say enough
when times got rough for me
to a point where I felt there was no return
you were always there to listen
an idea which at first spooked me more then life itself
for many reasons
one-my past experiences, two-my respect and honor for
you,
and most of all three-the thought of it possibly ruining
or even ending our friendship
one of which is very much wanted and appreciated
but after a while it made me feel at ease
we talked, choppy and hesitant at first
but then for some reason I felt at ease
and actually started to open up
again turning nervous because of the consequences
but you listened with an open mind
you did not critic or tell me how to handle it
you told me only how you'd be there
if I needed a friend to talk to
And in return the only thing I could say is
"Thank You"
but yet these words are not enough.
You've proven time and time again
true friends are more important then anyone realizes
you've always put them first
rearranging your schedule for them

yet the only thing you get in return is
"Thank You"
While we talked many things came out
things I thought were locked up forever
but things that felt good to finally get out
I never told anyone all that I had told you
and I appreciated the chance
I do still have closed doors
but thanks to you I do not feel as confined
atlas I have started to get things out
things that desperately needed to surface
yet the only words I say are "Thank You"
I do now feel guilty
that I unloaded a lot of problems on your shoulders
while you already have enough of your own
for this I'm sorry
I'm praying what I said does not change us
I'm hoping also with everything you know
that you do not treat me like a special case
that is also a big fear
but with all the help and support you gave
all I came up with is "Thank You"
You were right in one aspect
entering your room with things to say
yet leaving your room with the same things unsaid
We talked about a lot and mindless me forgot to say
what I was really there to say
you picked up on this
yet still did not get upset
I do not know what to say to thank you enough
so what do I do, I say
"Thank You"

I am grateful for the fact
that for the first night in weeks
I fell asleep stress free
Now when I feel at the lowest point in my life
I can look back and say it is not that bad
my life is great
because I have the privilege of knowing you
You'll never realize how much I respect you
the honor I have reaches higher then the clouds
but for me the greatest thing in the world
is to have the ability to call you friend
"Thank You"

Anything More

You know she'll always be there.
Is that what scares you so.
You talk, joke, and do many things;
but yet she still scares you,
not in a spooky way,
but in a secure sense.
You really like her
but yet talking is all you'll do
to scared to do anything more.

You're Sorry

Wanting to tell her
you're sorry
because you really are,
but the moment is never there.
Nights you dream
about how perfect it could be,
but you are too scared to say anything.
You lye awake at night
wondering
if anything could ever come from it
or if it is just a dream.

What Do You Do

What do you do
when you feel so much,
but you don't know how to say it?
How do you tell her
you love her
knowing she may
not love you back?
Is there a way
to change for the best?
She asks important questions
for you to answer
yet you know not how.
You answer the truth,
or from the heart,
and she's hurt.
You tell her
what she wants to hear,
and she's frustrated.
What do you do?

Seeing You

Seeing you makes me smile
makes me feel glad I am alive.
Your touch makes me
feel things I've never felt before.
Your kiss draws me
into another dimension
never before seen.
Maybe that is why
I am so afraid.
These are things I know nothing about
and it scares me.
These are things
that mean so much to me,
but to me
I do not know how she feels.
We talk,
but I 'm to, scared to ask
because I'm afraid of rejection
because no one could love me.
I will always
be a loner.

Why

Why is it that
you have so much to say,
yet say nothing.
Thoughts are present
you even plan how to say them,
but when face to face
you coward out
you run.
When she asks
you still hold back
unsure if what you answer
is what she is looking for?
Why can't you just say it,
just tell her,
but you can't
you were programmed
not to.

Being There

Being there is a step
in the maturing of someone
a step into the experience
of adulthood
a step
in the right direction.
The direction in which
is healthy and helpful.

Running Through Your Mind

Love is supposed
to be able to concur all
to overcome all evil
all temptation
why then does it not.

Tears form
with the reason unknown
you feel like crying
but you are not sad
you are not happy
you; well, there is no feeling
Tears form
as the thought
runs through your mind.

Smile laughter
are always present
tears appear
of joy and happiness
of anger and pain
brushed to the side.

Explains Why

Looking at this woman explains why other women are jealous
this woman with a figure of gold fragile and worth protection
her feet delicate and petite, her legs smooth yet razor sharp
piercing every mans thoughts
her waist slim, sexy, and one region hard not to notice
her slopes seductive, her neck ready to be bitten
her face with a glow of delight, her eyes sensuous and loving
one gets lost in oceans of imagination just looking into her eye
her lips luscious and very seductive with every word
she speaks one is drawn in closer to drool over what is seen
her hair golden brown curls of silk hanging downward
illuminating a face of beauty, this woman an angel in disguise
looking at this woman explains why other women are jealous
her tongue is free and loose, it lets out whatever is on her mind
she's honest and sweet, yet says what is on her mind
she walks with poise, a sort of cockiness
saying look there is no one like me so take notice now
the only problem is many do.
The way she walks so seductive and eye-catching
wiggling from side to side with slow strides for all the catch
she also plays coy
tries and succeeds in getting them to come closer
into her good view before she speaks
then the words no matter how cruel
sounds so sweet and sensuous coming from her
one also knows when she has past
the aroma of sweetness held in the air
as well as the trail of gold essence everywhere
this woman is more then any man can handle
the one man that does ever settle her down
will be the luckiest man alive
because knowing her is a very high honor
but to be her man one can not have an honor any higher
but beware, harm her and your life is over
this is a sexy sensuous woman, one not to be reckoned with
this is a woman of prestige, a woman of perfection
an angel.

More Pressure

You feel like you are
about to explode,
but yet you know not why.
Memories, ideas, dreams
all come together
without time in-between.
You feel like you are being squeezed
with no way out;
the pressure builds and builds
to a point you want to scream,
but you don't.
Things settle down
then reappear latter
only to add more pressure.

Angela

This afternoon
the wind whispered
your name
A-N-G-E-L-A
as it gently squeezed by
leaving a chill run
throughout my body.
An unforgettable chill.
A feeling I thought
had left me.

Steven J. Schuette

Aimlessly

Sitting there
one hour, two hour, three hour more,
but where did the time fly to.
The conversation runs nowhere,
but yet the comfort
feels overwhelming.
You notice so much
about the one you are talking to,
yet you never knew before.
Feelings flourish;
where did they come from,
why are they here.
your eyes opened to the reality of things
why did this not happen before.

The Median

Anger frustration
as it builds inside
is like claws
scraping inside you.
One day everything is so clear
the next
all is a mess.
Where does one find
the median,
the place
of ease and comfort.

Thanks to You
Traci

Thank you
Really you've
Always
Caught the hidden
Information

Giving
Enduring
Neutral
Generous
Luscious
Enforcing and
Retroactive

Advice
useful in many ways
to talk to you
makes all my problems and fears
set aside, yet I wonder why.
Feelings of
ease and admiration surface
as do wonder and glory.
Talking to you is worth more
then the world itself.
Thank you
is still the only thing
that I can think.
So from the bottom of my heart
Thank You

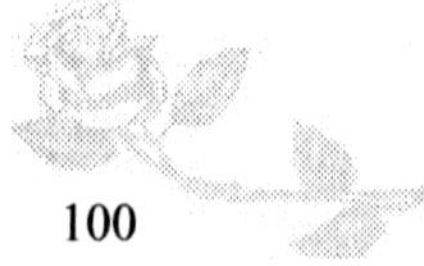

Reba

Reba
wow, who would have thought
a woman with such grace and poise
yet such ordinary, everyday kindness
Such a lovely name
belonging to a person who deserves it more
then any woman I know.
Reba
such a short
yet distinguished name
a name meaning so much
kindness, security, loving, caring, gentleness,
but most of all
a name meaning friend.
Reba
short for Rebecca
such a sturdy, structured name
fitting for such a person
a person who fits the name
in every way.
Reba
a person always willing to help out
always there
she's the person
with a shoulder to cry on
that person to hug
or that wall to talk to
but no matter what mood you're in
her smile will always
put anyone in a cheerful and enthusiastic mood
ready to concur the world
Reba
a name only a person like you
could ever posses

A Special Name

Paula is a name
that is always the same.
Sounds really nice
just like the roll of the dice.
You see it in a book,
and you just take a look.
You think it's the best,
but it's only a mental test.
The name is a treat
just so sweet.
Sweet as a flower,
straight as a collar.
The name never changes,
only has ranges.
From Paula to Paula
only when you calla.
Well that is it
time to quit.

Cassie

So sweet and innocent
so kind, loving, and gentle
a woman
with a smile
which enlightens everyone's day
her support
given in such a sophisticated way
she knows what to say
and when to say it
just to strike a little chuckle in everyone
her voice so soft, comforting, and enjoyable
this woman's name
is as lovely as the woman who bares it.
Cassie
a name so soft to one's ears
yet carries much with it
honor, trust, sophistication.
Cassie
always willing to lend a helping hand
always willing to be that brick wall
or that teddy bear in times of need.
Cassie
a woman always there to lighten one's spirits
to help a troubled heart
to lend friendly advice.
Cassie
in which to know is an honor within itself.

Melinda

The words
'Thank you"
can not say enough for all she has done,
for all she has changed, for all she has helped,
and for all that she has made better.
This sophisticated, gentle, and intelligent thing
with her delicate hands
holding the world high on her shoulder.
This woman is the right hand for some,
the helping hand for others,
and the hard hand for those few.
This woman
always ready to put others before herself
giving up her time to help a friend.
This woman
carries herself with grace and poise
as she crosses the room
presence of royalty, perfection, devotion is sensed.
This woman
strong enough to conquer the world
yet graceful liked a beauty queen
dedicated like a watch dog
yet gentle like a baby
giving so much to others
asking nothing in return
how can the words
"Thank You"
ever be enough
for this woman.

A Name

A name tells so much,
its personality,
a meaning,
the life,
and so much more.
A name can be that person's life.
A person may live,
live to fulfill his/her name
and then their life
may actually be passing them by.
The meaning of one's own name
should not run his/her life.

Beyond Our Understanding

We wonder what is out there,
what is beyond our sight.
What is to happen?
Not being able to see what is out there.
People talk about life from beyond our realm.
How can we accept this
when people can not accept
all that is on this planet.
Maybe we should open our minds
to what is right in front of us
before they are opened to what we can not see.

Jennifer

Woo Hoo
the two words that make everyone chuckle
makes everyone cheer up.
These simple words
come from such a complex person
complex in an explicit way
She's always willing to lend a helping hand
cheer others up with her smile stretching for miles
This woman with
short curly blonde hair
like hair from the gods
a voice soft and cushioning
one only fit for Jennifer
This woman always willing to talk
always looking for a way to cheer you up
always looking for a way to make you smile
Always there when you need her
When JD steps into the room
the fragrance of beauty and charm
sophistication, gentleness, and dignity are sensed
Jennifer is a woman
a woman one wants as a friend
because to be her friend
is one of the greatest honors
anyone could ever obtain
Listening to the wind whisper her name
so soft and gentle
makes one feel at ease and at peace with himself
knowing he has been honored
to know this one and only
Jennifer.

Gotta Love Me!

Lisa
a woman whose beauty
and sensuality is portrayed
all over her face.
Her eyes gleam
with the sparkle of crystal,
like the dew
on the morning grass.
A woman who carries herself
with dignity and grace.
A woman who knows many.
This is a woman that
not to know is death,
but to see once
needs a double take
just to realize
that the beauty you saw
is reality
and not a dream.

Robin

This woman
professional yet charming
well-done yet innocent
dignified yet flamboyant
a woman one should never double cross.
a woman whose friendship means more than life.
The honor of knowing this woman
reaches higher than the sky ever could.
This woman
sensuous yet stern
loving yet brutal
lovely yet strong
one trusts, believes, and wishes they could be.
A woman whose smile touches your heart.
This woman
short yet tall
tempered yet calm
uptight yet relaxed
A woman
whose golden hair makes you feel rich
whose green-blue eyes, makes you relaxed
makes you peer deep into her soul
A look so innocent and pure
a face so delicately designed
a face of a beauty queen.
This woman
who owns the name of such
a delicate and sophisticated animal
This woman could only be
the one and only
Robin.

Steven J. Schuette

Water's Beauty

Water has the beauty of life.
It breathes and speaks
to whomever is listening
to whoever wants it to.
Its color shines
with the happiness
it holds,
with the happiness
it provides,
with the happiness
it gives.
Water has the beauty of life.
Only you can realize
that beauty.

Names

A name so sweet
yet so cruel.
Where does the name come from?
Why do people
pick such odd names
and others pick such
precious names?
Why why why,
is the only question
left to ask.

Teri

Sly and sophisticated,
yet graceful
and intelligent;
charming and sweet,
yet ordinary and dignified;
caring and tough,
yet stern and helpful;
A friend whose there no matter what
ready to lend that needed hand.
Ready in a flash
always making you smile
no matter what mood you are in
always there to cheer you up.
Teri is the one
when a friend or a shoulder is needed
she's always sympathetic and supportive
she knows what to say and when to say
just the right words
to make you smile.
Teri's there
when things get tough
when a friend is what is needed.
Teri is the one
if you know her not
you are the one missing out.
Because to know her is to love her
as well as
to know Teri
is an honor of the highest kind
in which anyone can possess.

Tiffany

Sly and slender,
yet gorgeous and desirable;
stern and sexy,
yet rude and crude and indescribable.
"Peaches where are you?"
Questions asked without a reply.
Wait a minute!
Then you become aware
of a fragrance beyond belief
and you turn around to see
a beauty queen on her opening entrance.
You first notice the contours of her cheeks
the smoothness of her face
and the clasping eyes.
You ask yourself if this is a dream.
Please then do not pinch me.
Or have I died and gone to heaven.
Then she replies
in her melodious voice
one of perfection and harmony.
"Yes Hun"
and you melt
with the sweetness of her nature
and the warmth of her sincerity.
Then she crosses with grace and sophistication
only to have you thank God
that you know this woman of perfection
this gorgeous person
this person named
Tiffany

This woman

A woman
whose name is like daggers in your side
trying to be nice
and get it only shoved back down your throat.
Try to be honest and get ragged out.
Try to show your emotions
and get unprofessional criticism.
How on earth did this woman
actually get where she is today?
She's conniving, demeaning, and inconsiderate.
She's abusive of her powers and untrustworthy.
She's always looking over your shoulder
to make sure you are not out doing her,
but in reality that is not difficult.
To be in a position of power one should trust,
but this woman is neither.
She just snuck into her position
a position of prestige
one of which she has already ruined.
She's very rude, and yells at you
when if she just thought of it
she is also at fault.
This woman is lazy and undesirable
finding words to fit this woman
arrives at rude and crude meanings
there is not a nice word to describe this woman.
Patience is a virtue, but not for this woman.
A woman of double crossing standards
A woman not of her word
A woman unprofessional and unreliable
A woman
who it takes more than life to get along with
A woman or better yet
A DEVIL!!!

Steven J. Schuette

Sunset

The beauty of a sunset
so sweet
so colorful
so wonderful
and yet so informative.
The cooler
wow! what a sight.
The beauty is so
so
there are no words
for its beauty.
The wonder of why
why all the colors,
why does it come at a certain time,
why well who cares why.

Pictures

A Picture is worth 1,000 words.
It is a reminder,
a show,
or even a trophy.
A picture
tells a story,
holds a reminder,
and is worth more
then anyone can ever imagine.

Sexpot

A sensuous sensation comes over your body
as the letters roll succulently off your tongue.
The one with the body of silk and touch of heaven
when touched feels you've died and gone to heaven.
A touch you wish would never end.
A woman with hair of gold soft and sensual
curly like the motion of two bodies
together in such passionate and never-ending....
Someone whose eyes pierce to your soul
revealing all you inner desires and emotions.
Her eyes iridescent like her beauty
her eyes blue like the ocean
with waves crashing in onto my heart.
Blue like the sea calm as can be
blue like ice freezing us together forever.
With luxurious lips sleek like a stretched limousine
where the view, never-ending,
mesmerizing the masses like the flame of a hot fire
stoking passion from within.
With a chin which points out
one of the best qualities of what she possesses.
The face is a place
in which men's gaze becomes lost forever.
A woman with a neck so appetizing and juicy
as to a vampire.
Whose mountainous attractions is that from the gods
given only to a woman of such godly presence
a pure reflection of the goddess Venus.
A perfect image which makes any man melt at the
thought.
A sight which makes any woman merely jealous and
envious

A sight which makes any man wish she was his.
With silky legs stretching for miles
a sight men never forget, a sight men never want to forget
A woman whose feet so delicate and tender
just as she so small and sensuous gentle and kind just as
she.
A woman in which it is an honor to know
and yet even more of an honor to call her friend.
A woman whose name says it all.

Water

The blue green color
of a ruffled surface
so strange,
and yet so beautiful;
so odd,
yet so sturdy.
The water
is something everyone knows of,
everyone can relate.
The coolness, warmth, and the smoothness
of the water
is unforgettable.
The color, the waves
The water always has something.
Something to look at,
something to listen to,
or is there something to hear?
Yes! The crashing of waves,
the movement of the color.
The beauty of water
is in what you see or hear,
or in how you see or hear it.
No one can tell you
really how beautiful
it is.
Only you can say
water has the beauty of life.

Steven J. Schuette

Leave Me Alone

A woman
whose name drives a man insane
whose voice annoys most
a man's choice whether to listen or not
whose hair is snarled and ratted
one only dares to stroke through it
whose body is cranked and used
who'd want to be her or even with her.
This woman young and free,
annoying obnoxious
she's there, but yet she's not
uh ah are the words heard
'ZZZZZZZZ"
are then heard
is she worth it, am I good enough
why can't she handle me
maybe I am too much
maybe she's not worth it
but why can't I let go
why can't I ……
The woman
wanted by others yet glued to me
I say "good bye"
She says you're not leaving
can I not live my own life
why must she order me around
isn't this wrong
isn't this imprisonment
if I say it's over will she leave
or will it bring her closer
all I want is to be free.
A freedom from her is all I want
She's evil and vindictive
are all that's left to say.

Sheldon

Helpful and trustworthy, brutal and backstabbing
obnoxious and annoying, reliable and reverent
a man to know
a man never to double-cross
where on your side is a blessing in disguise
when an opponent you'd better be ware
he's tough and stern
ideas of his are thought out and thorough
with all minute details
so if you say he's wrong you'd better be ware
Honest yet recipient
he's there when needed
he goes out of his way to help, yet unappreciated
they say he snuck his way in
but he's got more class than most
so why then do they hate him
he thinks he's paranoid, but why
well things said, rumors are heard
right or wrong no one knows
but then why do they believe them
they know him not yet judge him by what others say
before judging him get to know him first
but getting to know him is rewarding, and stressful
but yet you gain more than a friend
you gain insight, support, and a gentle hand
you gain intellect, trust, and honor
because knowing him and being called his friend
is more than an honor.

Steven J. Schuette

Friend

Why is it so hard to say what should be said?
Ideas and thoughts run through my mind
yet none are good enough to show this woman what I mean.
One says say thank you or tell her she is great;
but she is more than great, and thank you is just not enough.
She was there when times were rough.
She is that soft voice to make me realize that I was wrong,
that shoulder to cry on, that wall to yell at,
that teddy bear to hug and never let go,
and the best of all that friend I can bet my life on.
Talking to her makes me realize
that this is a real woman one in every sense of the word.
She knows what to say at exactly the right time
truth, reality, Intelligent, reasoning
are a few qualities she possesses
yet remember these are only a few of her many talents.
Her smile can ease a troubled heart,
her eyes can calm a raging sea; her voice can tame a lion,
her kindness can….
well there is no comparison to her kindness.
Yet she never ever realizes that this is really true
But she will say "Yeah Right",
and never believe this herself,
She is stubborn, but still no one can compare
to a woman with the prestige and poise
of this woman.
Thank you is still not enough, but it is the best I know.
Thank you for all the time we talked
and you put my heart at ease; for every time we hugged
and I never wanted to let you go; but thank you most of all
for giving me the greatest honor
of being able to call you friend
not only friend though, but my friend.
You will never realize
that what I just said is true in every way,
but that is okay because to be able
to call you friend is the greatest honor ever

Traci G

This is a woman
who walks into a room
with the fragrance of beauty and charm
lighting everyone's spirits by her presence alone
One word form her lips
melts every man's being
a miracle, a goddess
beauty from head to toe.
Hair of golden silk, soft and free
eyes of piercing tranquility
cut right to one's soul and grab hold
lips of luscious love
sinuously grabbing your attention
a face of an angel
legs of heavenly beauty
that stretch up to the sky catching men's gaze
feet of delicate femininity small and fragile
these few parts outline
the magnificent, heavenly, succulent centers untold
this person
an outline of sensuous beauty
with a personality unmatchable
A woman where one glance is never enough
one glance only is a dishonor
A woman whose voice is of angels singing
A woman whose humor puts a smile on all faces
A woman where words are never enough.

"U"

This poem comes from the heart
to a woman who put a cushion around my heart
and when it broke she was there to glue it back together
a woman whose delicate face
relaxes a man at one glance
whose gentle eyes show a way to her soul
a place judge free, a place of harmony and joy
a place to hide in without any criticism
these same eyes peer into your soul
bringing things out
that you thought were hid forever
a woman whose words
are so soft and kind, supportive yet forceful
words that are trustful, yet soothes ever shaky whim
this woman ready with a helping hand
yet never asking for anything in return
someone you talk with, share many secrets with
slowly at first
with sweaty palms shaky knees
but one word from her makes everything calm
her kindness and understanding overflows
she listens and responds
with words you never expected
yet you tell her of your problems
and she understands
you ask question
thinking she will sway the answer
yet the truth is all you get
feelings you had long ago come back
is this a rebound or something else
feelings grow stronger
the security I once felt is gone

are these feelings just for that reason
or are these the ones I felt before
when we met there was something I felt
I threw it aside; I was dedicated to my promises
was I wrong to ignore it
we talked and it was easy to open up
Why not before when I did try to open up
got the door slammed in my face so I clamed
my problems grew worse and worse
but out of the whole mess
one person, one name
carried me safely through
this person was my shoulder to cry on
my support, she was my comfort
my kick in the butt, always there
judge free and never criticized
and these feelings were present for a second time
this woman strong as an ox
mentally and physically gorgeous
with small feet, delicate hands and a brain to outwit most
if these feelings are right am I missing out
would she ever, could she ever
if things don't work out
I'd hate myself for ruining her life
but what if they do work out
I am scared to take another step
I am scared not to
these feelings I have are to strong to ignore
in the past she'd tell stories
of what others did to her and I'd feel angry
I was jealous and upset, I knew she deserved better
should this have been a sign

maybe, but at least I know one thing
these feelings won't disappear, I must face them
all I can say is I am scared
and worried about what will happen
would she ever, could she ever
could we ever.

Nights

The night held mystery close
while fog lingered.
The quiet of the night
disrupted only by the few.
Lights shine their rays
only to affect those nearby.
Faint sounds drift in
Only when the sun comes out
does the fog give up its reign.
Leaving only memories

Thinking

Sitting there thinking
thinking
Boy! I wish I knew
what I was thinking.
Ideas, thoughts, reasons
pop in and out without prior notice.
What is a person to do?
Too many ideas pop in at once
sending your mind astray.
Confusion, frustration
which one why both?
To hard to make a decision,
to clear a thought.
Oh well, no one is perfect
present, part, or even future.

Music

Does music tell a story,
or does it have a meaning?
Well, music is a way of
love, expression, and entertainment.
A way of speaking,
but not literally.
Loud or soft it means the same.
Understood by some,
and hated by others.
Musicians show how,
why, or what they feel.
But do people know
how hard it is to say them literally.
Music can sound so
sweet, lovely, and relaxing
brutal, hard, and hateful;
but behind every song there is a message.
A message of some sort
Some people receive it,
and others have no idea about it
For those music is probably
for entertainment and/or relaxation.
Something to listen to, but no more then that.
That is fine
Music is for the person listening to it
It is then up to that person
to either get the message or not.
No one should force anyone else
to listen to one kind of music
Everyone should have his/her own
freedom of choice of music.

Jewel

The color of a jewel
makes it look so awesomely cool.
The shine, luster, and color
reminds me of my mother.
Small, compact, and sweet
it's always so very neat.
Always placed on top
just as a gravestone rock.
Perched above all
held above all.
Looked at.
Stared at.
Seen by whomever
seeming so clever.
Bringing back memories
good and badies.
Always that luster
reminds me of a cluster
of thoughts and ideas
that remind me of mamma mia.
The color is so nice
just like a block of ice.
So this just shows
that everyone knows
how precious a jewel is
even a dizz.

Steven J. Schuette

A Candle Flame

Flickering in the dark
making its mark
on the wall
so nice and tall.
Orange and yellow in color
like no other.
Spending its life all alone
just like a stone.
Only waiting,
and waiting,
for someone to end its life
with one swift strike.
Ending it for now,
and everyone knows how.
Only until the next time
when they think it is fine
to begin its life again
only to end and start over again.

A Unicorn

The soft, shiny, beautiful hair
of these wondrous animal
just illuminates it
just shows the total beauty.
The long sharp slick magical figure
it bares proudly on its head.
This figure, known as its horn
is so intelligent, and so distinguished.
This is the one thing that separates
the horse from this animal.
The figure is so built and defined
that all know what it is
A unicorn
no one can argue that.

On Your Own

Walking through crowds
feeling everyone is watching you
you begin to feel queasy
the thought of doing this
on your own
no one there to hold your hand
to talk to
to calm your nerves
only you
leaving on an adventure
new to you with no company
the not knowing begins to build
only till it is no longer together.

Steven J. Schuette

Dreams

Dreams
what do they mean?
Can they tell the future
of yourself or someone else?
Well only you can answer
questions like that.
Dreams
good or bad,
reality or imagination,
night or day?
Everyone dreams for many reasons;
boredom, pleasure, fear, physic, etc.
Dreams
visions or fantasy;
do I know?
Well only I can answer.
A dream
is what you make of it.
A dream
is special
to you only if you want it,
known
only if you tell,
important
only if you make it.
A dream is
A DREAM.

Unicorns

Unicorns so beautiful yet so unrealistic
so mind-boggling yet so understanding.
Unicorns
are they real or imaginary.
It is up to you
the person.
If you believe
then they are real.
If you do not believe
then they are make-believe.
Unicorns
your thought
or mine.

That Innocence

You look at her as if to scold.
She looks back with the face of innocence.
How can you be mad
looking at that face.
As if scared to death
she scowls as if to say
please no I did not mean it;
I just couldn't help myself,
I won't do it again.
You think does she know,
so innocent so young;
yet devious and mischievous.
Innocence like that
is hard to scold.

Steven J. Schuette

Excitement Flows Through

Sitting there
able to see what's happening
yet no movement
excitement flows through
the little body as if to say
me me play with me or hold me
do something just don't ignore me
I'm over here
hey you pick me up
please pick me up
please, please
oh come on someone pick me up
okay their not listening
let's try noise
they usually come
help help help hey help me
you try to say
but do they understand
footsteps you hear footsteps
yeh yeh yeh
here comes someone
over here, over here
I want out of here
you can just see someone coming
hey I'm over here
come here faster
they approach
at that time excitement flows through
that tiny little body
like a bolt of lightening.

A Feeling of Relief

A feeling of relief flows
as she stares up at you
as to say "I'm sorry".
"Please forgive me".
Your heart melts
as the sight of the innocent face.
You reach down
as if to say it's ok.
She gets excited to see movement
like a rush of relief flows through her.
She waits for you to pick her up
as to say "You're Forgiven"
and "I still love you".
As you hold her
the excitement subsides
as ease, calmness, and peace enter her.
She snuggles in
as to say
"I love you too"

Out

I jump up
to see if anyone is out there
but I know
I am too small to see out
but hey what the heck
I'm up
hey wait I can see out
I'm big now
I am a big girl
just like they have been saying
I want out
hey there help me out
I want to see
what else I can do
now that I'm big
Someone get me out
I need to explore

My Family

Schuette

Sound, Caring, Humorous, Unique, Enthusiastic, Thrifty, Thoughtful, Ebullient

Sensitive to all in need
Courageous in all situations
Honor is something we hold
Understanding is how we benefit
Enjoying life day by day
Trust is what we strive for
Tender is our heart, and
Everlasting is our love

Strong in all that is done
Done with compassion, love, and grace
Open eyes, which can calm unsettled seas
Installing much laughter in all we know
Always there in the time of need and always caring
Generous in all that is thought
God gave a gift, hope and trust
Compassion added to all that endure

Calming the raging fires in the hearts of others
Always trying to be optimistic
A person where thank you is never enough
This is kept between all and you
Great appreciation for the gentle hand and support you give
A friend who's there no matter what
Bringing smiles to all an impressionable heart
And gracious in all that is done

James F. Schuette

Jubilant, Awesome, Mighty, Energetic, Secure
Faithful,
Sensitive, Courageous, Handsome, Understanding, Eminent, Thoughtful, Tough, Educated

Just one word by him demands respect, demands attention

Journeyman in mind and
A great craftsman at heart
Majestic in what he does
Enlightening in what he says
Strength, courage, patience, generosity, and optimism

Five words that barely begin to describe him

Justice for all he knows
Love always in his heart
He's always there in time of need for all
Ready to jump in for whenever help is needed
Only to lesson the stress of others

Strong in ideas

His name begins with J
Leaving behind his saga
Strength above all is captured within him
A person that to know is a privilege
His soft-spoken words bring out the power he holds

Mary E. Schuette

Majestic, Authentic, Reliable, Young,
Eloquent
Strong, Creative, Hard-working, Understanding, Expecting, Tender, Tough, Enlightening

Memories everlasting

Marvelous in everyway
A woman whose presence brings smiles to gloomy faces
Reassuring voice which can tame a ferocious beast
Young at heart now and always

Enlightening is a word that explains her

A wonderful woman of brilliance
Whose words combination form one person
Her humble nature brings smiles to serene hearts
Yet no matter the time of day she always outdoes herself

Serene in all she does, thinks, and feels

She is a site, a picture, a form
Of a woman, this woman which depicts a
Woman of joy, strength, presence, and honor
Of laughter, friendship, love, and family

Jeffery T. Schuette

Just, Energetic, Family-oriented, Friendly, Enthusiastic, Rational, Youthful, Talented,
Safe, Craftsman, Handy, Upholder, Earnest, Thankful, Team, Equitable

Justified in all that he does

Judicial in all situations
Enlightening in all he says
Fair in all judgment
Funny at all times
Everlasting in all he loves
Reverent in all his thoughts
Young at heart

The one person who supports all

Journalistic is all that he knows
There to lend a helping hand
To share his free mind, his touch, his voice
To all or anybody (friend) there who listens
To anyone in need always ready to jump in always
Full of love and energy
And smiles to show he's happy

Showing he is enjoying life

Family friends and uses his **J**
To be just and fair for everyone
Putting family before all other stuff
Always working daily in turf
Always there to lend a helping hand for sure
An important volunteer firefighter
Never to leave and go away

Heidi J.A. Schuette

Honest, Elegant, Important, Divine, Impartial,
Joyful, Awesome,
Sensitive, Capable, Hopeful, Unquestionable, Endearing, Travel, Trustful, Empowering

Holding the world

High on her shoulders
Enjoying every minute
Important in all day to day judgment,
Decisions, and problems that arise
Impacting the life her and her family

Joying every moment
A friend who's there no matter

Handy in all she encounters
Which is encouraging to people
Empowering people's individual thought
As the day begins to come from the defeating darkness
And the sun begins to glare in your I

Sure to concur

Fulfilling all hope and dreams with a sigh
Today, tomorrow, and all time
Spreading her love out to all like jelli
Proven time and time again that a friend
Is important to all especially you and I

Paige R. Schuette

Patient, Altogether, Intelligent, Generous, Energetic,
Rational,
Shy, Charming, Honest, Unrivaled, Eloquent, Tranquil, Tidy, Eager

Persistent in all she has and will do

Pretty is a sight you will see
Anxious to grow up yet
Intelligent enough to know not to rush it
Generous to all she meets and
Everlasting is the hope she brings

Radiant everyday of her life

Patient to her is a virtue
Friends and family are number one
For a woman so intelligent as she is
A person always there giving a helping hand to all
Willing to stand by no matter the circumstance

Sure to seal the hearts of men

Always kind and in a snap
Is there to help out with no hidden agenda
Educated and charming is what comes to the I
Talent is what she, this young
Person has on her side

Emily A. Schuette

Eminent, Magnificent, Imaginative, Laughable, Young,
Awesome,
Soldier, Cute, Happy, Unique, Emphatic, Tremendous, Tough, Enchanting

Energy that supersedes every one

Elegance to catch the hearts of men
Making people smile even when upset
Imagination that surpasses all
Love for all she knows
Yet she is tough and strong

A person where others are put first

Each day living to the fullest
Making many friends along the way
Leaving pain anguish out of her life
Intelligence and strength will benefit her
Youth that keeps her lively

She's there helping others in their time of need

Lending that helping hand whenever possible
Currently the chance is slim
That she will be bored, but her I
For detail will
Be her strength surely and truly

Andrew R. Schuette

Adventurous, Navigator, Daring, Reasonable, Energetic, Worthy, Reassuring,
Sound, Courageous, Hearty, Undivided, Emulate, Trustworthy, Technical, Enthusiastic

A person that to know is special

And to have as a friend is an honor above all
Non-judgmental and caring to all
Daring in every situation
Ready to step in when help is needed
Ensuring his strength and gentleness
Wanting to lesson the stress on others

Reassuring others of their own strength

Able to make a smile appear
His soft-spoken words bring out peace and
All of the power he holds in his presence
Strength courage patience honor and prestige
Five words that just barely begin to describe this person
A person with love in his heart today and tomorrow

Sensitive to all in need

A great craftsman in his heart and a
Gentle hand in which he has given
Open-minded in all that is heard
Yet no matter the time of day or
The amount of pressure
He is always there never too slow

Dawn M. Schuette

Docile, Adaptable, Wonderful, Neighborly
Mother
Sincere, Cautious, Honorable, Unoffending, Enjoyable, Tidy, Tame, Enable

Depicting a woman of joy, strength, presence, and honor

Defines a – this woman
Adaptable in any situation
Who's humble and serene
Nature, brings smiles to impressionable hearts

Magnificent in all she does

Demanding nothing in return
Installing in you laughter beyond your imagination
Perfect strong look you will see and angel
Someone of grace love a woman

She is always outdoing herself

Always ready to take on the world
With eyes that calm a ragging sea
A heart full of love for which will show
Compassion for which there is no compassion

Alexander J. Schuette

Authentic, Loving, Encouraging, Xpressive, Acquired, Noble, Daring, Enthusiastic, Rambunctious,
Joyful
Safe, Changeable, Handsome, Unhesitating, Enlighten, Tender, Tame, Electrifying

A young soul ready to begin

Appeal its age now and forever
Loving his family newly and strongly
Everlasting love and endurance
Xpression lying on his face
And trail throughout his entire body
None of which ever stops moving
Daring to be unique, one of a kind
Enduring any pain or anguish it endures
Realizing the change now and yet

Justly deserving all that comes his way

A person with a strong mind
Never leaving an idea unturned
Always enlightening the people around
Making the holiday, **x**-mas exciting and lively
With his presence, noise, face, and movement
Keeping spirits of others around high and dry
Making others smile and laugh and brighten up
His voice calms a mother's loving heart
To know that he is still here around or near

Showing to all the strength he holds

Strength with no attached agend**a**
A mind that is straight and level
Someone always there
Abbreviated by the name Alex
Who needs support and **a**
Helping hand, but one thing know**n**
Is that his trust is never ending, but needs to be acquire**d**
One who will always be there
In the time of need now and foreve**r**

Haley A.M. Schuette

Hopeful, Awesome, Loving, Eventful, Youthful
Altogether, Majestic
Sincere, Caring, Honest, Upholding, Educated, Typical, Team, Ebullient

Honor is something she holds

Hoping one day to use it
Aware of the strength it possess
Leaving behind the fear and
Enlightening all that she sees
Yet patiently waiting for that time to come

A friend there through all
Making the meaning of a true friend real

Her words bring joy to hearts
Always installing kindness in others
Her strength and intelligence will benefit her
While her hand gentle with all
Will never leave or go away

Sincere in all she does

Facing each day without a sigh
Instead with great joy and a
Loving smile being respectful
To all around in order to give
Them a glorious day

Steven J. Schuette

Sincere, Tender, Educated, Valiant, Elaborate, Noble,
Just,
Smart, Creative, Helpful, Understanding, Educated, Thinker, Technical, Efficient

Strong in all thought and ideas

Strength above all is captured within
This person of intelligence and creativity
Enough to share with all around
Very understanding and tender to the feelings of others
Encouraging others to expand their abilities
Non-judgmental and caring to all

Journey man in his mind

Strong, sincere, and patient
Ready to jump in whenever needed
A person to where thank you is never enough
But knowingly is very appreciated
Making the meaning of true friends real
Living life in true appreciation

Sensitive to all in need

To all that endures
God gave a gift of hope and trust
Intelligence, creativity, and purpose
Being as the main objectiv
Of day to day life
For every person

Rebecca C. Schuette

Rational, Educated, Beautiful, Eloquent, Courteous, Cautious, Angelic, Child-hearted,
Self-confident, Charitable, High-spirited, Untiring, Erudite, Teaching, Talented, Eminent

Riding the wave of life

Reassuring all that everyday will be better while
Enjoying the time of others
Being most important in her life
Everyone including family, friends, and neighbors
Charitable to all in need
Creative in all situations
Angelic in all that is viewed

Calming the raging fires that burn in the hearts of others

Reliable is everything that comes out of her mouth
Open minded in all that is seen and heard
Smiles easing a troubled, aching, hurt, and very loving heart
Installing creativity, well there is no comparison to hers
Always ready if need be to take control of the situation
Keeping the enjoyment and learning combination
Available for all with no pre-made agenda

Strong in her convictions

There is no comparison to her
She is lively and a true angle
With no comparison, being superb
Gracious in all that is done
Like a kid energetic
And yet loving and romantic
With eyes that will calm a wavy sea

Terrence M. Schuette

Terrific, Eager, Remarkable, Resilient, Enjoyable, Negotiator, Courageous, Encouraging
Marvelous,
Strong, Calm, Hardworking, Undaunted, Effective, Tenacious, Thrifty, Equal

The one person where an action

Tiny as can be, can save
Everyone who is listening
Ruler of the house
Relying on everyone around
Even courageous looking forward to the future
No matter how hard or long it may be
Calming the hearts of those who are impatient, and
Everlasting in the love he has to give

Mighty, ruling with a fist

There to share with all in need always
With gentle hands to hold you close feeling safe
Yet possessing strength enough to keep harm away
Capable of expressing charm, hurt, love, and understanding
There to lend that needed talent and time
With the presence of a lion and a newborn kitten
There when needed most with patience and comfort
Using the life long tradition of everlasting knowledge

Strength, honor, and glory all combined into one

A friend who's always available no matter what
Keeping confident all that he will see
A man to brilliant for
Thought to really ever
Capture or mind to hold his statute
Just one word said by him demands attention
Disobey or ignore could be tragic
Yet always there for you and me

Lori A. Schuette

Loving, Objective, Radiant, Intelligent,
Agreeable,
Serene, Courteous, Hospitable, Unruffled, Enduring, Thinker, Tranquil, Exceeding

Loving is her nature

Level head in all situations
Open-minded leading into all issues
Rational in all her decisions
Intelligent in that she thinks

A person who is quite

Laughable and kind at heart
Someone who to know is an honor
But to call friend is an honor above everything
She is a sight for a sore I

Sincere in all that she does

Making decisions or correcting problems with a level
Head, keeping her family as numeral uno
Running her life not like a soldier
And now using wc instead of I

Taylor F. Schuette

Tough, Anxious, Youthful, Loyal, Open-minded, Respectful,
Friendly,
Sharp, Champion, Heartily, Unite, Energetic, Tooling, Typical, Eventful

Tough enough to handle anything

That is thrown his way
A man in his youth
Yet anxious to get into adulthood
Letting nothing stand in his way
Or at least doing his best not to
Reverent in all that he does

Friend until the end

There ready to help ready to share
And living a life of honor
In time of youth he is shinning
Living to the fullest possible
Sharing it with all of the people he knows
Now and in the future near

Strength abundant now and always

A child put through so much that
Being open-minded with no written agenda
Living his life day by day
Trying to obey and listen in order to be respectful
And to gain respect from numeral uno
His family, friends, father, and mother

Dakota J. Schuette

Daring, Active, Knowledgeable, Open-minded, Tough, Aware
Jubilant
Strong, Cautious, Hearty, Understanding, Ever-lasting, Tender, Thoughtful, Energetic

Down to earth with a mindset of peace

Defining a person
Always there in the time of need
Knowing just what to do
Offering that needed support
Though his words or deeds
And wanting nothing in return

Just in all thoughts

Daring to be strong
through all turbulance this world has offered
The time is here knowing that in mind
Showing he's ready to jump in
With spoken words that will bring out the power within
This man holding inside With **a**

Strength, honor, prestige all combined into one

Anxiously awaiting his adulthood
With no hidden agenda
Trying to find that next **K**
Yet always on the go
Yet containing a heart
That is as peaceful as the sea

Gross

Genuine, Respectable, Objective, Sound, Smart

Generous in all that is thought
reliable in all that is said
open-minded in all that is heard
strong in all that is done
sensitive to all in needed

God gave a gift of hope and trust
honor, time, and knowledge
to everyone who is around
strength and compassion were added
to all that endures

Always there in the time of need and always caring
yet no matter the time of day or
the amount of pressure they're always on the go
always outdoing themselves
calming the raging fires in the hearts of others

Steven J. Schuette

Lawrence H. Gross

Laughable, Aware, Wonderful, Reverent, Educated, Navigator, Cautious, Eventful
Happy
Great, Reassuring, One, Swift, Strong

Love always in his heart

Level in a judgments
And compassionate in all thoughts
Who looked from thoughtful eyes
Realizing the changes throughout
Ensuring his strength and gentleness
Navigating his way through life
Caring for all less fortunate
Even for those he did not know

Honor is something he possess

Looking for the good in everyone
With family and friends above all
He is always there when needed
With honor and patience
There to lend a needed talent and time
With a presence of a newborn kitten
Always there with some comfort
Using lifelong knowledge

Gracious in all he does

For detail will
Always be left in his saga
For everyone to know
That he was here and for
All the gracious things he has done
The gentle hand he has given
Always trying to be optimistic
And just and fair to everyone

Cynthia D.L. Gross

Caring, Youthful, Neighborly, Trustworthy, Honest, Intelligent, Authentic
Divine, Loving
Glorified, Respected, Open, Sincere, Self-confident

Ceasing the day with

Courage above all
Yet learning day by day
Not knowing when to start or when to stop only
There to show the path to others with
Her will unnerved
Impacting the life of others
Always aware of the future

Doing it with compassion, love, and grace
Lending that helping hand wherever needed

Calming the pains of other
With Only the thought of them in mind
Being non-judgmental for every situation
Bringing smiles to many of there impressionable heart
Calming the unsettled sea with her open eyes
Leaving the anguish out of their lives
Leaving behind ideas and a lifelong saga

Generous in all that is thought

Always trying to be optimistic
Even in the worst of tragedy
Showing to all the compassion
She holds within her heart
A person that feels it's never enough
Always there for you and I
With a grade of an A

Aaron L. Gross

Awesome, Authentic, Reliable, Objective, Nowledgable
Lighthearted
Gracious, Rational, Optimistic, Strong, Smart

Always willing to lend a helping hand

A person that to know is a privilege
and to have as a friend is an honor above all
ready to jump in when help is needed
only to lessen the stress on others
non judgmental and caring to all

Love is always in his heart

A person where thank you is never enough
strength above all is captured within him
his spoken words bring out the power he holds
strength, courage, patience, honor, prestige
five words that barely begin to describe this person

Great appreciation for the gentle hand and support in which you
give

A great craftsman in his heart and a
journeyman in mind, leaving behind his artifacts and saga
one word and all obey all honor
no temper, no anger, no
just one word said by him demands respect, demands attention

Lori A. Gross

Loving, Objective, Rational, Intelligent
Altogether
Generous, Reliable, Open-minded, Sensitive, Secure

Love always present in her heart

Loving smiles which can ease a troubled heart
open eyes which can calm a raging sea
reassuring voice which can tame a lion
installing kindness, well there is no comparison to hers

A friend who is there no matter what

Look, you will see an angel
perfect, loving, beautiful
always ready to concur the world
this is kept between you and **I**

Gracious in all that is done

Makes the meaning of true friend real
strength, honor, and glory all combined into
one who installs in you laughter
keeping you spirit high and dri

Jacob A. Gross

Jubilant, Anxious, Courageous, Optimistic, Brave
Authentic
Gracious, Reasonable, Objective, Sound, Sincere

Justice for all he knows

Judicial in all situations
A great thinker at heart
Creative in all he does
Objective in how he thinks of others
Being most important in his life

Able to make a smile appear

Just be one thought or one action
Courage always in his heart and mind
Always ready to take control if the situation needs
Sharing it with people he knows
no comparison, superb

God gave a gift

To this person beginning with a J
With a heart full of joy and a
Mind yet loving and romantic
Keeping family and friends as numeral uno
He is with no comparison, superb

Peter J. Gross

Patient, Enlightening, Tough, Energetic, Respectful
Joyful
Grand, Radiant, Onward, Sensitive, Soldier

Patient with all around

Persistent in all he does
Enlightening in what he says
Thoughtful in all he completes
Everlasting in all his compassion
Reverent in all his thoughts

Joyfully perusing each day

Putting family above all other
Empowering people's individual thought and
no matter the circumstance willing to stand by
Ready to jump in whenever needed
And knowing he is still near

Generosity known by all

With the will to help
And the support to endure
With an encompassing heart
And the mind of being sure
Showing what he has, honor

Printed in the United States
830000001B